AF598989

DEER HUNTING

BY SAMANTHA S. BELL

childsworld.com

The Child's World
childsworld.com

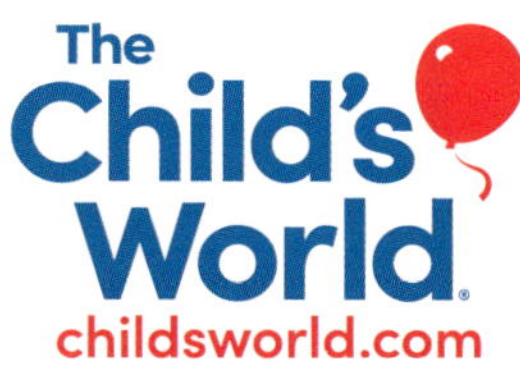

Published by The Child's World®
800-599-READ • www.childsworld.com

Photography Credits
Photographs ©: Richard G Smith/Shutterstock Images, cover, 1; Shutterstock Images, 5, 14, 21; Musa Visual Media LLC/ Shutterstock Images, 7; Tom Tietz/Shutterstock Images, 8 (top); Tom Reichner/Shutterstock Images, 8 (bottom); Nikolay Gyngazov/Shutterstock Images, 9; Jim Cumming/Shutterstock Images, 11; iStockphoto, 12, 13; Jeffrey B. Banke/ Shutterstock Images, 17; Light Field Studios/iStockphoto, 18; M. Arkhipov/Shutterstock Images, 19

ISBN Information
9781503869714 (Reinforced Library Binding)
9781503880986 (Portable Document Format)
9781503882294 (Online Multi-user eBook)
9781503883604 (Electronic Publication)

LCCN 2022951132

Printed in the United States of America

BRINGING THE WORLD TO YOUNG READERS 1968

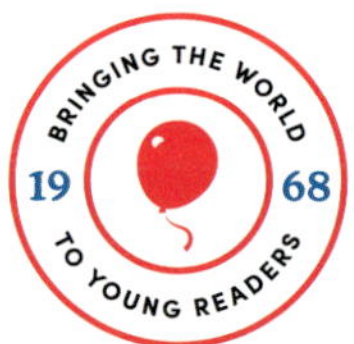

ABOUT THE AUTHOR

Samantha S. Bell has written more than 130 nonfiction books for kids. She lives with her family in the foothills of the Blue Ridge Mountains, where they spend a lot of time enjoying the wild outdoors.

CONTENTS

CHAPTER ONE

DEER SEASON

Taylor grabbed her blaze orange cap as she headed out the door. The crisp fall air made her shiver, but she didn't care. It was the first day of deer season, and she couldn't wait to go hunting with her dad. She loved watching for deer in the woods.

When they reached their destination, Taylor and her dad slipped on orange hunting vests. Now other hunters would be able to see them easily. Then they headed to their favorite hunting spot.

Taylor and her dad set up their double tree stand. It had two seats about 12 feet (3.7 m) off the ground. They attached the stand to the trunk of a large tree. They put on safety harnesses before climbing the stand. At the top, they had a good view of the area. Today, Taylor and her dad were bowhunting. They got their bows and arrows ready and waited.

Suddenly, Taylor's dad nudged her. He pointed to a doe, or female deer, walking nearby. Taylor carefully raised her bow and pulled back the arrow. The doe came closer. Taylor let the arrow fly, but it missed the deer. They watched it bound away. Taylor sighed, but her dad smiled at her. The woods were full of deer. She'd get another chance.

Deer hunting requires patience and planning. Hunters must stay hidden and keep quiet to make sure deer don't get scared off.

HUNTING TIME

Each state decides its own dates for deer hunting season. Most hunting seasons start in early September and run through December, but some last longer. The dates are based on the number of deer in the state and the health of the herd. Healthy herds have deer of all ages. If there are fawns, or baby deer, it means the herd is breeding. If there are older bucks, it means the herd has enough food to live to old age. A larger deer population means a longer hunting season.

For kids like Taylor, fall means more than the start of school. It also means the start of deer hunting season. In the fall, deer born in spring are old enough to live on their own. This means that if hunters shoot a mother deer, young deer will still survive.

Another reason for hunting in the fall is trophies, or animals for display. Bucks, or male deer, grow new antlers in June and shed them in January. In fall, their antlers are the biggest they will grow that year. Some hunters display the heads of these deer. The trophies remind them of the hunt and show off their success.

Deer are the most popular **game** animal in North America. The main groups are white-tailed deer and mule deer. White-tailed deer include eastern white-tailed deer and Coues deer. Mule deer include Rocky Mountain mule deer, Columbian black-tailed deer, and Sitka black-tailed deer.

Many trophy hunters target bucks with big antlers. They sometimes mount the heads of the bucks on walls as decoration.

Many people hunt deer for their meat, called venison. An average white-tailed deer can provide about 45 to 68 pounds (20.4 to 31 kg) of venison. Some hunters and their families eat venison. Others donate it.

Hunters can identify different types of deer by looking at their tails, ears, and antlers.

Many people enjoy hunting with family and friends. Older hunters can share their love for hunting with beginners.

For many people, deer hunting is not just about getting deer. Hunting helps them appreciate wildlife. They enjoy spending time outdoors and connecting with nature. Others build relationships with family and friends while hunting.

CHAPTER TWO

Deer Hunter's Checklist

Before going deer hunting, people must decide where the best land is. Most deer live in forests, which provide them with food and hiding places. Skillful hunters study the **terrain** of forests, looking at fields, trails, and **ridgelines**. This helps them locate deer.

People have several options for hunting locations. They can hunt on public land owned by the state or national government. In some places, hunters must pay a fee to hunt. In others, they can hunt for free. Some hunters buy or rent land for hunting.

If a hunter isn't using his own land, he needs a hunting license. Hunters buy licenses from the state where they want to hunt. Every state has different requirements for licenses. Sometimes people must take hunter education courses before getting licenses.

Deer hunters can use guns or bows. Each state has rules about when these weapons can be used. Some hunters add scopes to their weapons. A scope makes faraway objects appear larger. **Crosshairs** on the scope help hunters hit their targets.

Most types of deer in North America are found in forests, prairies, and meadows.

Hunters should practice aiming accurately so they can make a clean shot. This makes sure that a deer suffers less when it is shot.

Hunters can choose from different kinds of firearms. Rifles are the most popular type. They are more **accurate** at long distances. Shotguns are better for shorter distances. Muzzleloaders are guns loaded from the front end with only one shot. Using this type of gun makes a hunt more challenging.

Hunters can also use different types of bows. Traditional bows have one string that a hunter pulls back. Compound bows are shorter and have more strings. This type of bow allows hunters to hold the string longer and make more accurate shots.

Some bowhunters use 3D targets to practice their aim. The targets are made of foam and look like deer.

On a crossbow, the string is already pulled back and set in place. This way, hunters won't scare deer away with extra movements.

Hunters should be able to shoot accurately with their weapons. Many hunters practice at shooting ranges, or places designed for gun training and practice. Young hunters can join shooting camps, youth shooting leagues, or 4H clubs. These programs teach kids hunting skills and give safety tips.

Some people hunt during winter when deer are usually less active. To stay safe in winter weather, hunters should wear warm coats, hats, and gloves.

It's also important to wear proper clothing for hunting. States usually recommend wearing bright orange or pink hats, shirts, and vests. This way, hunters won't mistake each other for deer. The bright colors help prevent accidental shootings.

Hunters should also wear comfortable layers to keep them warm in the early morning hours. As the day warms up, hunters can remove layers. **Insulated** boots also help keep hunters warm.

Some hunters hunt from blinds, or small structures on the ground in which they can hide. Deer may come close enough to give hunters a clear shot. Other hunters wait for deer in tree stands. These often have ladders and seats for one or two people. Some hunters use binoculars to spot deer from far away.

COLORFUL WORLD

Deer have excellent night vision and can see colors, but not the same way people do. Deer can see blues and greens about 20 times better than people can. But their eyes don't pick up on reds and oranges. This means that deer can't see a hunter's pink or orange clothing. But they can easily spot someone wearing blue jeans.

CHAPTER THREE

HUNTING RESPONSIBLY

Many people enjoy deer hunting, but it can be dangerous. Sometimes injuries happen. Many accidents involve hunters falling from tree stands. Stands are typically 15 to 30 feet (4.6 to 9.1 m) off the ground. Hunters can fall while climbing up there. They might lose their balance or fall asleep in a stand.

A hunter using a tree stand should always wear a safety harness. The harness has a strap that fastens to the tree. If a hunter slips or falls when she wears the harness, the strap catches her. Hunters should practice climbing stands, especially in the dark.

Even when hunters wear bright clothing, accidental shootings sometimes occur. This can happen when hunters do not receive enough training. Before hunting, a person should know how to use her weapon safely. She should make sure it works correctly and know how far it shoots. A hunter should also be aware of what is behind her target and where other hunters are. She must always treat her gun as if it was loaded.

A hunter should make sure his safety harness is on correctly before climbing up to a tree stand.

Kids and beginners should take hunting safety courses before their first hunt. They should always go hunting with an experienced adult.

Hunters should come prepared with snacks, water bottles, and first aid kits.

Education programs teach hunters how to use weapons and other equipment safely. These programs help reduce the number of hunting-related injuries. But hunters should still be ready for emergencies. They should always bring a first aid kit when hunting. They should also bring a whistle, radio, or cell phone in case they need to signal or call for help.

Hunters must also know the bag limit, or how many deer they are allowed to kill. These limits vary from state to state, ranging from one to six deer. Bag limits may change based on location.

A HIDDEN DANGER

Most bullets contain lead, a substance that is harmful to people and animals. When deer are shot, the lead from a bullet can get into the meat that people eat. To prevent this, hunters should avoid shooting deer in the hips and shoulders. Hitting the bones in these areas can cause pieces of lead to scatter and spread into more of the meat. Deer remains may also contain lead. A hunter might shoot a deer with a lead bullet and then leave unwanted parts of the deer behind. Animals that eat **carrion** may swallow the lead in the deer remains. Many become sick and die. Nonlead bullets are an option. But they're expensive and often unavailable.

For example, specific areas within a state might have different bag limits. Bag limits may also change based on the hunter's age and the type of weapon used. They can depend on whether a deer is a buck or doe, too. In some states, hunters must report each deer they kill to a state agency. This helps states keep track of the deer population.

Bag limits help manage deer populations. If the bag limit is too high, too many deer may be killed. The population might fall. If the limit is too low, there may be too many deer in an area. This can lead to vehicle accidents involving deer.

Becoming a responsible deer hunter requires training and practice. Hunters must follow the rules closely to stay safe. But with enough knowledge and skill, both kids and adults can enjoy a successful hunt.

Many states require hunters to attach tags to the deer they shoot and report their kills to a state agency.

GLOSSARY

accurate (AK-yuh-rit) To be accurate is to be exact or on target. A hunter must practice to become an accurate shooter.

breeding (BREE-ding) Breeding is when two animals reproduce and create offspring. If a herd of deer has fawns, it means the deer are breeding.

carrion (KAYR-ee-in) The bodies of dead animals that are rotting are called carrion. Animals that eat carrion help keep the environment clean.

crosshairs (KRAWS-hayrz) The two fine lines that cross each other on a scope or other instrument are called crosshairs. The crosshairs on a scope help hunters hit their targets.

game (GAYM) Wild animals that are hunted for food or sport are called game. Deer are one of the most popular game animals in the United States.

herd (HERD) A herd is a group of animals that feed and travel together. Deer of all ages may live in a herd.

insulated (IN-suh-layt-ed) When something is insulated, it is protected by a material that holds in heat. Insulated boots keep feet warm.

ridgelines (RIJ-lines) Ridgelines are lines that follow the top of a hill or mountain. Deer will often cross ridgelines at their lowest point.

terrain (tuh-RAYN) Terrain refers to the physical or natural features of an area of land. Studying the terrain of a forest can help hunters figure out where deer might be.

FAST FACTS

- In the United States, deer hunting season is often in the fall.
- Some people hunt deer for the meat. Others hunt to have a trophy animal.
- In the United States, each state has its own deer hunting regulations.
- Deer hunters wear blaze orange or pink clothing so other hunters can see them. This helps prevent accidental shootings.
- Deer hunters often use bows or guns. Other deer hunting equipment includes blinds and tree stands.
- Handling a hunting weapon requires a lot of practice. Many hunting accidents can be avoided if hunters have enough training.
- Hunting helps manage the deer population. Hunters can support a healthy deer population by following bag limits.

ONE STRIDE FURTHER

- Deer hunting helps manage the deer population. What do you think might happen if people didn't hunt deer?
- Many kids go deer hunting with their parents. Based on what you learned in this book, what do you think is a good age to start hunting? Why?
- For hunters to be able to keep hunting, they must help protect the environment where animals live. What do you think hunters can do to help protect the environment?

FIND OUT MORE

IN THE LIBRARY

Bell, Samantha S. *Firearm Safety.* Parker, CO: The Child's World, 2024.

Doyle, Abby Badach. *Deer Hunting.* New York, NY: Gareth Stevens Publishing, 2023.

Nayeri, Daniel. *The Most Dangerous Book: An Illustrated Introduction to Archery.* New York, NY: Workman Publishing, 2017.

ON THE WEB

Visit our website for links about deer hunting:
childsworld.com/links

Note to Parents, Caregivers, Teachers, and Librarians: We routinely verify our Web links to make sure they are safe and active sites. So encourage your readers to check them out!

INDEX